HENRY NAYLOR

Henry Naylor is a multi-award-winning UK playwright, who has been described as 'one of our best new playwrights' in *The Times*, 'one of our best new playwrights' in the *Evening Standard*, and 'one of the finest British writers on contemporary events' in *Theatre Extra*. Since he became a playwright in 2014, Naylor's plays have won or been nominated for thirty-three international awards, including one of France's most prestigious awards for the arts, the Globes de Cristal. In 2016, he joined J.K. Rowling in having written one of the 10 Best Plays of the Year by *The Times*. He is one of only a handful of writers to have won a Fringe First three times, and has won four of the top five Fringe awards at the Edinburgh Fringe, including the Carol Tambor Best of Edinburgh Award. The one he hasn't won – the Amnesty International Freedom of Expression Award – he's been nominated for twice. Three of his plays have had month-long runs off-Broadway, and in 2017 alone there were over three hundred public performances of his work, over five continents. His work has been translated into eight languages.

Borders is his fourth play. The three which preceded – *The Collector*, *Echoes* and *Angel* – have all been published by Nick Hern Books as *Arabian Nightmares*.

Prior to becoming a playwright, Naylor had been comedy writer, producer, director and performer, best known for his award-winning writing, and for working with comedy partner Andy Parsons in *Parsons and Naylor's Pull-Out Sections*. He was a lead writer for *Spitting Image*, and has written for many well-known, award-winning British TV and radio shows, including *Alas Smith and Jones*, *Dead Ringers* and *Alistair McGowan's Big Impression*.

Other Titles in this Series

Henry Naylor

BORDERS

NICK HERN BOOKS
London
www.nickhernbooks.co.uk

A Nick Hern Book

Borders first published in Great Britain in 2018 as a paperback original by Nick Hern Books Limited, The Glasshouse, 49a Goldhawk Road, London W12 8QP

Borders copyright © 2018 Henry Naylor

Henry Naylor has asserted his moral right to be identified as the author of this work

Cover image: photograph of Avital Lvova by Rosalind Furlong

Designed and typeset by Nick Hern Books, London
Printed in the UK by Mimeo Ltd, Huntingdon, Cambridgeshire PE29 6XX

A CIP catalogue record for this book is available from the British Library

ISBN 978 1 84842 723 5

How *Borders* Came To Be
Henry Naylor

Every writers' course I've ever been on, the teachers present writing as a calm orderly process. Methodical and logical. They plot carefully, using cork boards and coloured cards. Carefully structuring each beat, each arc. That, they will tell you, is how a script is written.

That's how to be a writer.

That's the way.

Borders was not written like that. *Borders* was written in a frenzy.

That's not to say that the arcs and acts aren't there; they are. But the process at which I arrived at them was ruddy chaotic.

The play was first staged at the Edinburgh Fringe, at the Gilded Balloon, 3 August 2017. I only started writing the show eight weeks before, in June. Rehearsals were in July. I'm always disorganised, a bit of a shambles. This was off the scale even for me.

The reason I wrote it so late? – I wasn't going to write it at all. I was going to write a play set during the Second World War. In February 2017, I had done six months' research into 1940s combat. Preparing to set pen to paper...

...when a series of encounters led me in a different direction.

At the time, I was on tour in Australia with my third play, *Angel*.

(*Angel* is the story of a displaced Kurdish sniper called Rehana; it tells a kind of modern-day 'Joan of Arc' story.)

The show was attracting significant following from the Kurdish community. We had groups coming almost every night. Some folks came and over again. One senior member from the community came five times.

Australia, being Australia, it was easy to meet the audience afterwards. We began hanging out, talked politics, were invited to Kurdish banquets, the New Year ceremony of Newroz.

Many of our new friends were refugees. Many had recently fled Syria. One even ran a settlement programme for Yazidi women fleeing the persecution of ISIS. They shared their horrifying stories. And universally expressed frustration that the Western Press wasn't doing more to help. There was a feeling that 'News Fatigue' had taken hold in the West.

Suddenly, I began thinking less and less about the Second World War, and more and more about the Syrian conflict.

I looked up the statistics. Since the death of the little boy Aylan Kurdi, over 8,000 people had died or gone missing in the Mediterranean. This was an urgent problem; a problem which hadn't been solved. And needed addressing now. The Press coverage was clearly inadequate. And The Arts were culpable too.

In New York: another formative experience. *Angel* was playing at 59E59. A senior figure at the UN – Maher Nasser – saw the show, started tweeting about it enthusiastically. We met up, he gave us a private tour of the UN (!), and he not only put us in touch with several refugees who'd just fled Syria, but also the heads of some refugee programmes.

Like John Messenger in the play, I felt it was imperative not to look away.

The decision was made. We would do a show about this urgent and pressing crisis… Working title *Borders*. But we had to do it fast.

Returning to England – before we really knew what the show was about – we had to take publicity photos for the Edinburgh Fringe photo. The picture on the front cover was taken by my extraordinarily talented mate, Rosalind Furlong. In her friend's hot tub.

I then teamed up with a long-time collaborator, Michael Cabot. He'd directed versions of *Angel* and *The Collector*. He knows how chaotic I can be – and has a calm hand. I needed it, to help guide me through the flurry of scripts.

I began writing all day and all night; once I even did a thirty-six-hour writing shift. Reading the script back now, I can see that the frenetic writing process has been reflected in the words, giving *Borders* an immediacy and an energy.

Next, as time was of the essence, Michael and I had to do the Casting… before the first draft of the script was finished. I'm aware that most writers don't do that. But that's normal for me. I like to tailor the lines to fit my cast. It creates a real Truth on stage. I also like to hear the script read back to me – it's an essential component of the editing process.

So, we picked Graham O'Mara from an open casting to play Sebastian. Graham's a well-known and respected performer on the London indie circuit. He was perfect for this role. He has the ability and experience to deeply move an audience – but also has superb comic-timing. In fact, he delivered the jokes so well, I wrote him more and more gags, and his part became increasingly comedic.

Avital HAD to be Nameless. She'd been there when I did my research. She'd been there when I met the dozens of refugees who had inspired the story. The research was unique, unparallelled. She'd also been an invaluable sounding board while I worked out the themes of the show, and is one of the best young actresses around.

The results were spectacular: her performance in Edinburgh was extraordinary. She managed to capture the essence of the refugees we'd met; masterfully capturing their strength and dignity – they had experienced humanity at its worse, and yet they demanded no pity. Avital performed a Truth that I'd rarely seen on stage before.

The show that emerged was unlike anything I'd written before.

As a writer, I've got a kind of schizophrenic personality. For over twenty years, I wrote comedy. Largely writing news-based satire – for *Dead Ringers*, *Spitting Image*, *Alistair MacGowan*, that sort of thing. But in 2014 I also started writing 'weighty' dramas (*The Collector*, *Angel* and *Echoes*).

Borders was the first time I tried to reconcile the two sides of me.

One character, Sebastian, would be largely comedic – satirising the degradation of 'news values' and the absurdity of celebrity culture. The other character – Nameless – would be more serious, and would attempt to put a human face on the Syrian crisis. I wasn't sure if the mix was going to work...

Borders would be a story about a lot of things.

It would be a story about how the West interacts with the East.

It would be a story about the twenty-first century so far. About Bombs, Bono and Bin Laden.

It would be about how, since 9/11, the West has become increasingly insular – and how we've become callous towards those suffering in the East.

And it would address the identity of 'Art'.

The show was so last-minute, the ink of the script so wet, that the cast barely knew their lines at the tech run. We were still playing with the ordering. We had three journalists scheduled for our first performance... I feared a disaster.

The first hint I got that things might be okay, was when my old friend Steve Ullathorne gave me the thumbs-up. Steve's a magnificent photographer and always takes production stills at the Gilded Balloon's techs. He was the first person to see *Angel* – and now the first person to see *Borders*. He's also a very honest guy. If the show was shit – he'd tell me.

God bless him, he loved it.

And I loved all the shots he took too... with one caveat: all the pictures he took of Avital Lvova showed her scowling, as she spent the whole tech run being pissed off with herself, for forgetting her lines!

The show ended up doing better than we could have hoped. It sold out every single performance, and got twenty-one four- and five-star reviews. It won the Carol Tambor Best of Edinburgh Award and a Fringe First, was nominated for the Amnesty International Freedom of Expression and The Holden Street Theatres Awards.

It's been touring internationally ever since. At the time of writing this, we've just come back from Australia – and South Carolina, New York, Cape Verde, Amsterdam and Moscow are round the corner.

And there may be more touring soon.

Sadly, the show remains relevant. The refugee crisis still haunts us – in the first 108 days of 2018, the International Organization for Migration report that over 18,575 migrants have had to cross the Mediterranean – a tragedy which has barely registered with the press.

The headlines of the papers today are, instead, all about Meghan Markle's father...

H.N.
May 2018

Borders was first produced as part of the Edinburgh Festival
Fringe at the Gilded Balloon Theatre, Edinburgh, as a Redbeard
Theatre/Gilded Balloon Production on 2 August 2017. The cast
was as follows:

SEBASTIAN NIGHTINGALE	Graham O'Mara
NAMELESS	Avital Lvova
Director	Michael Cabot

The script was rewritten for the Australian premiere at the
Holden Street Theatre, Adelaide, on 12 February 2018, with the
same cast directed by Louise Skaaning.

Borders was then performed at the Spoleto Festival in
Charleston in May 2018 and at The Theatre Next Door at New
York Theatre Workshop, New York in June–July 2018, with the
same cast, directed by Michael Cabot with Louise Skaaning.

Acknowledgements

There are almost too people to thank here. Besides, I didn't always catch everybody's name, particularly in the early stages, when I was still writing a Second World War play! But I would like to say a few especial thanks to: Sherko Kirmanj, Khadija Abbas Kate Kirmanj, Jwan Abbas, Kamal Xder, Burhan Zangana, Riham Alkoussa, Maher Nasser, Sana Mustafa, Yousif Murad and Danny Dougramachi who were especially generous with their stories, their hospitality, their contacts and their time.

I'd like also to give huge thanks to the Gilded Balloon team, and the Korens: Karen Koren, Katy Koren and Kristian Koren. Also my PR people-extraordinaire, Paul Sullivan – and in Australia, Neil ward and Angela Tolley.

A massive shout-out to my artistic collaborators – Avital Lvova, Graham O'Mara, Michael Cabot and Louise Skanning, and the many technicians we've worked with (especially Ashley Smyth).

I'd also like to thank the photographers Rosalind Furlong and Steve Ullathorne for bringing their creativity to the show.

Sean Gascoine, Amy Sparks and Nicki Stoddart from United, and Lou Coulson and her Lou Coulson Associates team, have been brilliant.

So, too, have the artistic directors and presenters we've worked with around the world: Heather Croall and Nick Phillips of Adelaide Fringe; Martha Lott and the Holden Street Theatres Team; Joao Branco of Mindelact; Iri and Emma Vitorgan in Moscow; Elske Van Holk and Dora of STET; Nicole Taney and the Spoleto Festival team. And in New York: Carol Tambor and Kent Lawson of the Carol Tambor Foundation, Yang-Yang and the rest of The Theatre Next Door team. I'm also hugely indebted to Nick Hern Books – especially to Sarah Liisa Wilkinson, Matt Applewhite and Nick himself – for helping to put this book together. Would also like to thank Viv and Leo, obviously. And Phil Goodwin – who's been a massive help at various stages. And finally, the biggest thanks of all my wonderful team at home – especially my magnificent and uber-smart and beautiful wife, Sarah – Deb, Phil, and my mum.

H.N.

To V & L

Characters

SEBASTIAN
NAMELESS

SEBASTIAN. Balochistan, March the 5th 1998.

The valley beneath, a religious experience. A landscape for
arks. Trembling with menace and liquid fury.

Those aren't rafts beneath, they're roofs. Those people aren't
waving, they're pleading.

The noise of the rotors, violent; their shiver demanding
fast film.

But I have long put down the camera.

Instead, on my stomach, looking down the length of a fishing
wire, hauling on board our latest catch: a farmer. His eyes
hollow. Dripping mud and fear.

I try to pull him on board, but he won't let go of the wire or
his terror.

Paramedics prise his fingers off the cable, his family
chittering, relieved, excited.

But the farmer has no emotion.

His spirit, gone, carried away on the torrent.

I have saved six lives today. But this one, won't join the
living.

Only looks down at the hopeless floodwaters.

Must busy myself with my lens choice. Must capture his
hollow look. The human face of disaster.

Suddenly, the family's cries distant beneath the violence of
the rotors.

I look up: the farmer's gone.

Has thrown himself spinning to his death in the waters
beneath.

Not even a ripple in the flow.

Lights up on NAMELESS.

NAMELESS. Homs, Syria. March the 5th, 1998.

The playground in our street.

Fierce sun, turning the sandpit, into an instrument of torture.

But even aged six, my compulsion to draw is too great.

I'm drawing Simba, the orphaned lion cub in the crust.
My father admiring. 'You should be an artist when you
grow up. You've a good eye.'
I'm glowing in pride.
Suddenly he stiffens.
There's men in the playground. Big men with unkind faces.
Blocking every exit.
'Shabeeha' – the secret police.
Turns to me – (*Urgently*.) 'Remember: Just stay true to your
vision. Never follow anyone else's lines.'
A bald-head thug approaching; bumps the swing.
Which writhes and twists on rusting chains.
'Run,' whispers Dad.
Heavy bootprints in the sandpit.
RUN!!!!
Running, running.
Behind: my father's final shouts of defiance.
The lonely swing. Contorting. Creaking with pain.
Me, Six, crossing the border from childhood to adulthood.

SEBASTIAN. I'm twenty-one. Fresh out of uni.
Determined to change the world.
I have the talent, the vision to be one of the world's leading
photojournalists.
To raise awareness of the Poor and the Suffering...
As soon as someone buys my pictures.

No one buys my pictures.
Balochistan barely features in any of the papers.
Where it DOES, it's buried so deep, it's among the chairlift
adverts.

Now, back at the hotel in Islamabad, I'm Broke. And too
proud to phone my father for more funds.
Am guiltily loading the complementary fruit platter into
every pocket. Knowing it would be my evening meal.
Someone sees my bulging pockets, says: 'You only need
five-a-day, not thirty-five.'
It's John Messenger. THE print journalist of his age.
'Bloody hell,' I say.

An apple drops out of my pocket.

'Helloyou'refamousI'vebeenphotographingthefloodsvictimsi
nBalochistan.'

'Have you now?' Messenger moves off with a plate of eggs.
But I follow.

'And how are the Balochistanis?'

'They could probably do with their own Live Aid concert.'

'What and inflict Bono on these people? Haven't they
suffered enough?'

I laugh too hard.

'How old are you?'

'Twenty-one.'

'Why you here?

'Didn't want to go into the city like my mates; wanted to do
something constructive.'

'Enjoying yourself so far?'

'I saw a man kill himself.'

'Ouch. My advice: Always keep the lens between yourself and
the action; got to protect yourself... Sold any pictures yet?'

'No.'

'So how's this financed?'

'My parents. Till I get established. Which I will; I take good
pictures.'

He tosses his fork noisily onto his plate. 'Being a good
newsman has nothing to do with Art. It's about being in the
right place at the right time. I'm not the best writer. But I was
there at Tiananmen; at the Wall...'

He pushes egg yolk round his plate. 'Want a paid gig? Need
a stills-man for an interview with a local warlord.'

Warlords are two-a-penny out here. It's almost harder to find
someone who ISN'T a warlord.

'What's special about this guy?'

'He's a billionaire. Launches missions from a cave.'

'Who is he? Batman?'

'They call him the Sheikh. His name: Osama Bin Laden.'

Lights and mood change.

NAMELESS. Don't ask for my name.
    Only the powerful have names.

Call me nameless.
Call me fatherless.
Call me what you will. But not my name. It's mine; it's all
I have left.

They took everything, when they took him. They took my
trust, my love:
They took my mother; was never the same again. Spent her
days praying.
And I lost my home.
We moved to an apartment in the Christian district, just so
mother could be closer to the Church.

I still had my Art. But they took the pleasure from it.
I drew, and drew obsessively – seeking to please a father
who wasn't there.

April 2011.
The clock has stopped. I'm winding it up, when my mother
enters from evensong.
'What do you want for your birthday, Mum?'
'Paint me a picture.'
'What of?'
'Something which lifts the soul. A mural for my bedroom.'
I put the clock back, the seconds-hand now beating.

The art shop in the Al Souk is small and rammed with paints,
colours, crayons. Creativity packed tightly like an explosive.
I wriggle. The shopkeeper and his son are squeezed behind
the counter like tubes of burnt umber.
'Hi. I need some wall paints.'
'If you want to buy aerosols you have to leave your details,'
says the son. Around my age, handsome. Knows it.
'Why?'
'Assad's clamping down on graffiti art. Since Dera'a...'
I roll my eyes.
He laughs.
The revolution here began when a kid sprayed anti-Assad
slogans on his school in Dera'a. Assad arrested fifteen
children. Removed their fingernails and genitals. The
country's been in revolt ever since.

'So are you a graffiti artist?'

(*Smiles*.) The question makes me feel dangerous. I don't deny it.

I pick up one of the Artists' Mannequins. Starting shaping it to my design.

'Am going to paint a mural. Was going to copy something from the Sistine Chapel. Michelangelo's *Creation of Adam*.'

'Ah. God the Great Creator, showing us how it's done. Striving with every fibre of his being to touch the soul of man. Nice. So. Do you really want to leave your details? The Shabeeha WILL read them.'

'No.'

Put the mannequin back. It falls on the floor. A painful mess of twisted limbs.

SEBASTIAN. You don't just turn up at a Warlord's house.

He comes to you.

We were picked up on a street corner.

Blindfolded, shouted at, pushed from vehicle to vehicle and subjected to an eight-hour journey from Hell.

Hard to imagine, unless you've flown American Airlines.

Finally, rough hands pull at our blindfolds.

Light: painful, fierce.

A goat track emerges, then Guards, staring with intense naked hatred.

One shouts, points at my bag.

I'm perplexed.

He mimes taking a photo.

Boots and hooves on the track.

Suddenly, round the bend, a man on horseback, flanked by eight warriors.

A carefully stage-managed event.

John smirks.

I whip out the camera: nail the focus; shoot. Hurriedly taken. But a career-defining photo. Everyone's seen it.

Bin Laden on a black horse, in cream robes.

NAMELESS. Creeping home through backstreets, am being followed.

A van. White: keeping a constant distance.

Shit.

Pretend I haven't noticed.

Add twists and turns to my route.

Can't shake my pursuer.

See a narrow alleyway. Too narrow for vans.

Bolt down it.

NO.

Dead end. Shit.

The van blocking the entrance.

Trapped.

The door opens.

Out steps the shop assistant.

'YOU??'

'Left your bag in the shop.'

'Didn't.'

He opens the passenger door.

A sports bag.

Inside:

Eight cans of spray.

'We need artists.'

'To do what?'

'To decorate the streets. Tonight's the perfect night. The Shabeeha will be busy at the demo.'

'Why you doing this?'

(*Eyes down, face scarlet.*) 'I'm nineteen. Next year's my military service. Can't do it; can't fight for Assad.'

'Sorry.' I turn to leave.

He says to my back: 'I'm Rifat. You are…?'

'Nameless.'

SEBASTIAN. Batman's cave is not what you'd expect.

Looks like a budget lawyer's office: Pine bookshelves, filled with tomes, thin rugs.

The Sheikh's keen to be seen as scholarly.

Wants to be photographed before the books.

Rests his AK against the shelves, angles himself towards the lens, cross-legged on the floor.

He's handsome, tall, photogenic. Mine's an easy gig.

John's isn't. The Sheikh's dull. Has all the charisma of a Town
Planning Officer.
He has no idea about pithy soundbites.
Simply lectures us about the brilliance of ancient ways,
whilst exposing a Casio digital watch.
Blah blah blah, the West is decadent and whoring.
Blah blah blah, the West never cares about Muslims.
Blah blah blah, we must have separation between the
communities.
I completely zone out.
Start looking at the framing.
It's all wrong. I need to get Bin Laden in closer relation to
the AK.
As if prompted by a force of telekinesis, the AK then slides
down the wall.
The Sheikh makes to stand –
But 'I'll get it' – Messenger reacts first.
Catches the gun.

And there's a moment.
A solid moment.
Which we all feel.
As real and as tangible as the floor beneath our feet.

Messenger weighing the gun in his hands.
'…Surprisingly heavy,' he laughs, nervously.
Then rests it back against the book case.

NAMELESS. Eight protestors shot dead yesterday.
The whole town demonstrating at Clock Tower Square.
Women, children, families.
Thousands upon thousands.
I normally avoid crowds. But this one can avenge my father.
'Not Sunni, not Alawite, Freedom is What We Want.'

A young man approaches.
'The Women must go, sister. There will be violence.'
I snort.
'Not Sunni, not Alawite, Freedom is What We Want,' I shout
back.
His friends laugh.

The police nearby. Silent.
The acid of fear eating at my gut.

Leave at 2 a.m., before the curfew.
Military vehicles and Shabeeha gumming up the
approach roads.

Am squeezing past, heading to the bus stop,
when the sudden sound of aircraft.
Everyone senses danger...
WHUMP!
A burst of red light. A thumping explosion.
The town erupts.
Machine guns.
Thunk-chunks of semi-automatics.
Screams.
Flashes from nearby rooftops.
Chaos of the crowds,
Bumping
Elbowing
Falling to the floor.
Sheltering in doorways.
Filming on phones. Everyone filming, everyone a
cameraman now.
Allahu Akbar.
Bang bang.
Running directionless.
My ears, blood thumping. Breath overpowering.
A screech of wheels.
(*Screams.*)
The bus stops. Doors open.
'Okay sister?'
Jump aboard. Others cram in behind. Puffing panting.
Doors shut.
Myself, the protestors. Grinning, relieved.
But turning a corner.
The driver brakes.
Concrete barriers. A roadblock.
A tank. Spotlights. Police.
Doors open, a policeman boards. 'You got activists on board?'

Driver shrugs.

Policeman addresses the passengers. 'We know who you are. Give yourselves up.'

Silence.

Sees me, the only woman onboard.

'Why are you out this late, sister?'

'Seeing my boyfriend.'

'THIS night?'

'Has something been happening??'

Now, his pistol between my eyes.

'What is your boyfriend's name?'

Mind blank.

The only name I can think of: Rifat.

'You love the President the same as Rifat?'

'Of course.'

He grabs my lapel. Drags me off the bus.

A picture of Assad on the roadblock. Grinding my face against the image. The gun against my temple. 'Kiss him. You love the President: Kiss him.'

So close I can see the pixels of the print. Face to face with my enemy. I purse my lips. (*Spits*.) Streaking the poster with saliva. The first defacement.

SEBASTIAN. A giant woodlouse scurries across the floor.

We're in the Royal Crescent, Islamabad. It's 1998; you can still buy alcohol – in the hotel bars.

Drinking heavily celebrating our escape from the World's most tedious terrorist.

'Fuck, he was DULL. He's the only person I've ever met who can make the destruction of Western civilisation sound like a dishwasher instruction manual.'

'Don't underestimate him. He beat the Russians. Destroyed an Empire. If he wants to drive a wedge between East and West, he'll do it.'

'Bollocks!! *Him??*'

'Were you thinking what I was thinking when he started talking about Holy War?'

'Were you thinking about doing unspeakable things to the cast of *Baywatch*?'

'No.'

'Then "no, I wasn't". Sorry, I'd zoned out at that point.'
'I seriously thought about shooting him.'
'So why didn't you?'
He shuts his eyes. I wait for his response. But he says
nothing, and I begin to wonder if he's fallen asleep, when
another woodlouse scuttles past.
I make to squash it.
But Messenger stops me.
'The woodlouse isn't the problem. Woodlice feed on rot.
To get rid of the woodlouse, get rid of the rot.'

NAMELESS. Prison is rammed. Must have arrested half the
town.
Am Questioned, Numbered, Crowded into a cell.
Can't all lie down, take turns to sleep.
Not that anyone can.
The animal screams of torture too loud.
A limp prisoner is thrown into the cell.
She has been hung by her wrists from the ceiling for over
a day. Women start massaging her forearms.
If they can't get the circulation going, she'll lose her arms.
Feel nausea.
This is what my dad will have experienced.

Next morning, I am fortunate. The prisons are overloaded, so
the women are released.
We're not seen as much of a threat. Ha.
Big mistake.

Rifat's waiting outside the jail.
'Need a lift?'
'What do YOU want?'
'You told them I was your boyfriend; they came to the shop;
checked out your story.'
(*Panicked.*) 'What did you tell them?'
'Why do you think you got released? Now kiss me, in case
they think you were lying.'
'Go and fuck your mother.'
(*Rifat laughs, purses lips.*)
Prison officers watching by the gates. Must go along with
the charade.

Put my lips near his and whisper 'asshole'.

We drive in silence.

Pass a tank, and a van full of Shabeeha.

'Want to show you something.'

Turns into a residential area. Points out some graffiti on a shop.

'One of ours.'

It's a disappointing stencil of a construction sign. The logo underneath: 'Caution: Democracy in the making.'

'Who did the design?'

'Downloaded it off the internet. Egyptian; used in the Arab Spring. Need volunteers to spray these around town. Are you in?'

'No.' It offends me. Artists have their own vision; they do not download designs from the internet.

'Get me a tin of red enamel paint… I can do better.'

Rifat changes into higher gear, smiling.

SEBASTIAN. Three years later, Southern Sri Lanka. Normally lush, tropical down here. Instead, parched earth like rhino hide. You can put your arm up to the shoulder in the cracks. Don't think that, because I'm here, my career has been a success.

It's not.

The work has dried up worse than this paddy field.

I've had to do wedding photos to supplement my income… The happiest days of people's lives: the most humiliating of mine.

The only reason I'm in Sri Lanka, is I'm on holiday.

And am only taking pictures in an attempt to convince the taxman that this trip is a 'work expense'.

The farmer doesn't know that. Says: 'Please, please: show this to the world. Things are bad.'

'Will try my best.'

But the brutal truth: won't get published until more people die.

Grubby and sticky, back at the hotel.

My father calls, anxious.

'Any luck?'

'Nothing anyone will buy.'

'You need Americans to go thirsty. That'd do it.'

'Yeah… YEAH!!! You're a genius.'

In New York, there's been a heatwave, which has killed four
people; if I can take some pictures there, combine them with
the Sri Lanka shots, I've got a photo-essay about global
warming.
I do the calls, get interest from the *Observer*.
So September 11th, 2001 I'm at Heathrow, heading to
New York.

Flight delays.
'What the fuck is going on?'
'You not heard?'
A fellow passenger nods towards a monitor in the Starbucks
opposite.
There's a small crowd watching a dreadful action movie.
A plane flying into a building. Far-fetched Hollywood bullshit.
I shrug.
My reaction surprises him.
'It's real.'
'FUCK. FUCK.'
'We are so lucky, if we'd set off twenty-four hours early we
would have been there.'
'I am so unlucky. If I'd set off twenty-four hours early, I would
have been there.'
Proof I'm not a newsman. NEVER in the right place at the
right time.
I kick my bag across the concourse.
'FUCK.'
My phone rings. John Messenger.
All I need.
'Long time no speak.'
'Don't tell me you're in New York.'
'Okay, I won't.'
'Where are you?'
'Huddersfield.'
'Huddersfield? Why are you in Huddersfield?'
'I'm not in Huddersfield, but apparently I can't tell you I'm
in New York.'
Bastard.
'Seen the news? Pentagon's gonna do a statement about the
mastermind behind it. There's only a half-dozen or so

Western journalists who've met him: You're one.'
'What, Batman???'
'*GMTV* wants someone who "knows the REAL Bin Laden".
Gave them your number. You got an agent? You're going to
need one.'

NAMELESS. Night. In Al-Adawia Park there is a golden statue
of my father's killer.
I've always delighted in the pigeons which shit on it.
They were Syria's first rebels.
Now it's my turn to join their revolution.
And soil Hafez al-Assad's image.

I flip the lid of the red enamel.
Brush in.
Drip drip, flick. Flick. Spattering the killer's gilded coat.
Painting fingers, palms, hands in gore.
Now annointing his bloody head.
Writing underneath. 'The Assads: Your Local Family
Butchers.'

Next day. Everybody's talking about it.
The park's shut for 'essential cleaning'.
For the first time, I sense Art's power.
I'm drawing my own lines.

SEBASTIAN. *GMTV*, the breakfast show, is to News what the
Crazy Frog is to Beethoven.
I'm about to be a guest.
And I'm disappointing the twenty-two-year-old researcher
from *GMTV*, who's prepping my interview with Eamonn
Holmes.
'What was he [Bin Laden] like?'
'Nothing to say, really: he was dull.'
My new agent snaps: 'Can't say that on television.'
'So what *do* I say?'
The researcher nibbles a hangnail.
'Okay. When I met him he was surrounded by these
intimidating henchmen.'
(*Researcher relieved.*) 'Good: mention them.'
'One had a scar. One had metal teeth.'

(*Researcher thrills*.) 'Oh. My. God.'

'And they led me to his high-tech office where he was stroking a white cat – '

'Oh, my!'

'And strapped me to a bench and pointed a laser at my testicles.'

'Really?'

'No.'

She attacks the hangnail. 'Please take this seriously. *GMTV* is a heavyweight news show.'

I mutter an apology. My agent hisses. 'Don't fuck this up.'

I'm led next to Eamonn Holmes, the heavyweight newsanchor.

On the sofa, I wear a haunted look, recount the eight hours in a blindfold, the Sheikh's evil determination, the AK against the wall.

Eamonn calls me 'very brave'.

Then I start playing to the camera. Give him the soundbite he craves: 'I met a Supervillain. He didn't have a freeze ray or laser gun. He just had an idea and a fifty-billion bank account.'

Eamonn almost orgasms on the spot.

Inside he's flipping the bird to the BBC and saying: 'Eat shit, *Newsnight*.'

When we finish, he says 'you heard it here on *GMTV*, first for hard-hitting news.'

NAMELESS. Rifat is annoying me: he volunteered for lookout duty, but he's watching me work. Chatting noisily.

'Never could paint, myself...'

Am in a moonlit carpark, painting a mural: the Eagle of Syria devouring the Dove of Peace.

'...I'm a great disappointment to my father: Art's his life...'

I would tell him to shut up, but one of his Network – a Plumber – got me past the checkpoints in his van.

(*Rifat*.) 'Am More of a Musician, really. Just wish my Art could be political, like yours.'

'All Art's political; just find a way to reach out.'

I step back, appraise my work:

I've come a long way. At first I did stencils, then cartoons:
Assad as Putin's puppet, that kind of thing.

Now: these grand murals.

A sudden wave of sadness, because it will be destroyed by
the morning.

Assad's People will spray over the work, write slogans
beside. The one place we debate politics in Syria: on
garage doors.

(*Rifat*.) 'A masterpiece.'

'No.'

'Yes. A good painter pleases the eye. But a Grand Master
touches the soul... That's you. You're like God the Great
Creator: straining with every fibre.'

Silence. I sniff as though Rifat's words are meaningless.
But I'm sure I'm glowing in the dark.

SEBASTIAN. Busy. Done twelve interviews in three days.

Recognised in the street.

Might be playing to the camera too much.

Created hysteria about Bin Laden's capabilities.

The *Daily Telegraph* carries an artist's impression of Bin
Laden's base, with hydraulic lifts, bunkers, a monorail.

I think the artist must be the set designer for *Octopussy*.

I've had my fun. Now, back to work.

But there's no disasters to cover.

I phone my agent: 'Any hurricanes? Exploding oil platforms?'

'What do you know about Daniel Bedingfield?'

'The singer?'

'His agent wants him to appear edgy. So he wants him
photographed by the man who shot Bin Laden.'

'Fuck off.'

'Am serious.'

'Not doing that. He's shit.'

'Never say never. See what they're offering.'

'Tell them I don't get out of bed for less than ten thousand.'

Phone down. There's talk of war with Afghanistan. Might
call a mate in the Army, see if I can get embedded.

The phone again.

'Didn't get ten thousand.'

'Well, thanks anyway.'

'Got fifteen.'

'For real??'

Then the doubts:

'I dunno… it's fucking Bedingfield.'

'Fifteen grand for two days' work? You can't say no.'

I can't say no.

In the words of Bedingfield: I 'gotta get through this'.

NAMELESS. 'Seems a nice boy.'

Mother's watching me paint God's straining fingers on the mural.

She's taking a vicarious interest in Rifat; since my father died, she's refused all male advances.

At the moment she's being pursued by a filthy mechanic called, Stinky Joram. He's a local personality who runs a garage and a crime ring.

'He's as much my boyfriend as Stinky Joram is yours.'

(*Mother shuddering.*) 'Your father was the only man for me.'

'Just as well. Or you'd have Joram's 'Greasy Engine'-fingers on your boobs. Eeew!'

(*Mother crosses herself.*) 'You can't talk like that: not in front of God the Father and Adam.'

I return to God's fingers.

Artillery providing the soundtrack to my work. The pecking of automatics, the thud of AKs.

Then: Music.

A sudden assertion of beauty against the insistence of battle.

Warm notes winding round pillars.

The sound of an oud.

Curious I slip onto the street.

Join others, feeding on the beauty like the malnourished.

See the musician: Rifat.

'Get under cover: Snipers.'

'No now, I'm reaching out.'

(*Rifat smiles.*)

This performance: for me.

Asshole.

We hug.

He tries to kiss me.

I slap him, laughing.

I look forward to him picking me up.
We talk about families. Dreams.
He's the only person I've told about my father
'Why did they arrest him?'
'Was an activist. Worked the front desk at the Al-Bab Hotel.
Nights, he'd secretly use the photocopier to print protest
leaflets. But one night, it jammed. Never realised a copy was
still in the machine.'
He squeezes my hand. I let him.

Night-time. Working the ruins of the Al-Souk district.
I hear the sound of spray.
Friend or foe?
Watch from a distance. See an artist I've never seen before.
Spraying a message.
I read: 'Assad Traitor.'
Friend.
I step out, say 'Ho!'
His glare, hostile.
'We're on the same side.'
I hold up my hands, showing the red tin of spray.
Movement in the shadows. Companions. Faces bandaged
black in scarves. With AKs.
The painter steps aside. Reveals the full message:
'Assad Traitor: The Caliphate is at hand.'
Fuck.
Jihadis.
One of them steps forward.
'Cover yourself, whore.'
Spits in my face.
Fucker.
Spray paint in his eyes like Mace.
He screams, face dripping red,
I run
Leaping over rubble.
Bullets crack.
Concrete sprays, left and right.
(*Screaming*.) RIFAT!
Tension of an engine.

The van
door opening
Get in
hollers screams
I'm in
reversing before the door's shut
flashes
a shower of glass
the windscreen gone.
Engine straining
The Jihadis shuddering into distance.
Clear.
Clear.
We're clear.

Pounding pounding Blood
'Shit, that was close.'
You okay?
Pounding
You okay?
Can't turn
Paralysed.

Stood at the lip of the abyss.
The Netherworld between this life and the next
Death's cold fingers in my hair
The breath of the void on my neck.
Serpentine coils
Constricting
Squeezing
Crushing
Fading
Fuck

'Breathe!
Breathe!'
Slipping
Slipping
'Fucking Breathe!'
Spinning
Swirling

Madness, a madness
A bray, a gasp, a heave of air
(*Breathing*.) I can't... I can't... (*Gasping*.)
The smell of flesh
An Urgency, an Instinct
To fight
Must fight
'Fuck me'
'Huh?'
'Fuck me.'
'But, but – '
Roaring
Biting
Tearing
Fighting;
Ripping
Clawing
Hissing
Mauling;
Burning.
Burning.
Elbows
Teeth
And Talons;
Savage and
Pouncing;
Gripping
And Forcing
the source of Life.
Inside.
Taking taking
And Taking –
With blood
and Bleeding.
Not sex. Not sex. Not sex.
Def-i-ance.

SEBASTIAN. I'm loving having Money. For the first time in
my life, I can take my father out for a meal. The shock nearly
gives him a heart attack.

I don't want to look like I'm showing off, but after the meal,
I order a sixty-pound bottle of port.

'This really isn't necessary, Sebastian.'

'Why not?'

'Because it's breakfast.'

'Got to live a little, haven't you?'

My phone rings: my agent.

'You wanted to shoot disaster areas? – I got you a corker:
Britney Spears.'

'What??'

'Wants to rebrand herself – do some glamour shots – while
she's still got a septum.'

'Rebrand herself as what?'

'The Girl-Next-Door.'

'To me, she already is the Girl-Next-Door. Mind you, I live
next door to a crack den.'

'You interested?'

'Well, you know, One "For-the-Art", One "For-the-Money".'

'One "For-The-Art", ten thousand "For-the-Money", more
like.

N-I-C-E.'

Put the phone down.

My father looks disapproving. 'What was that about?'

(*Faux innocent.*) 'What??'

'Hope you're keeping your standards up?'

'Oh yeah, yeah. Social Issue. Doing a picture feature on a
Single-parent mother with a drug habit.'

NAMELESS. Next morning everything aches. The tension of
the attack. The strain of, of THAT.

First thing I do, clean my underwear. Trying to wash away
the fact.

Prickled under the skin by the pins of shame.

I even pray with my mother. The mindless repetition, balm
for the troubled mind.

'You not going out tonight?'

Revolution can wait for a day.

But our work is important; I can't put off seeing him forever.
Hot with embarrassment and shame, I find the shop.

He's tender and angry.
'Where've you been? Thought you'd been arrested.'
(NAMELESS *shrugs*.)
(*Rifat*.) 'You okay?'
(NAMELESS *shrugs*.) 'Shaken up.'
Downtown, the thumping heartbeat of rotors.
So much to say, impossible to say it. He attempts small talk.
(*Rifat*.) 'Those Jihadis were worrying, yeah?'
I say nothing.
'They were very together.'
'Of course they are. They're here for one reason, whereas
Syrians have a thousand-and-one grievances.'
'Some of our team reckon our message is too messy; needs
to be more focused. I was thinking maybe we should work
together more. I mean, if we all used the same stencils...'
'I'm not doing any stencils??'
'Just saying, if we're going to defeat Assad, we have to
compromise.'
'Compromise IS defeat. I want to have the right. To be ME.'
'Can't fight this war alone.'
Anger rising, gunshots closer.
(*Rifat clears his throat*.) 'Anyway, I... Liked what we did.'
'"What we did" was stupid. This is no place to fall in love.'
'Do you think that we did was wrong? Would you prefer it if
we were married?... I mean would you...?'
'What???'
'...Be my wife??'
Suddenly I'm slapping him, screaming, and spitting like an
alleycat.
'Are? You? Crazy? Did you not hear? What I just said? Did?
You? Not? Hear? I work alone.'

He leaves gift boxes of paint outside the door.
Won't open them.
My mother brings them in.
'Be kind to the poor boy...'
But the Artist. Alone. Never compromises her vision.
Seeks no reward. No glory.
She draws her own lines.

SEBASTIAN. Bin Laden bought me a BMW and a deposit on a house.

The growth industries after 9/11: airport security, the military and Me.

Overnight, he turned me into THE celebrity photographer.
Bedingfield, Britney, then Will Young and the Black-Eyed Peas.

And now I'm Robbie's official photographer at Knebworth, the biggest live-music event in British history.

I'm there, taking post-gig pictures in the Green Room.

When suddenly, a face I recognise:

Johnny Messenger.

'You photograph Celebrities now?'

'Making hay, John: Married.'

'How much hay do you need? Did you marry a horse?'

(*Chuckling*.) 'What are you doing here?'

Points to a young girl, queuing for Robbie's autograph.

'Granddaughter's birthday. Press pass useful for something.'

'Nice one.'

'Going to the Philippines tomorrow. Typhoon Imbudo. Sixty-two thousand homes destroyed. Fancy coming?'

'Still doing this.'

'Robbie won't mind; he likes Charity.'

'Need to feed my family.'

'So do the Philippinos.'

'My wife wants a bigger haystack.'

Joviality fades; he grumbles off into the crowd.

I take a Jack Daniel's from a passing waiter.

Knock cubes of ice against the side of my glass, like conscience.

See the farmer, falling from the 'copter into brown waters.

Drowning in whisky and ice cubes.

Then the ice melts into nothing.

NAMELESS. Alone with my paint.

Seeking a smooth surface. Too many pockmarks, too much shrapnel.

The city powdered, the paint won't take.

I stand before defiant walls. And curse. And curse.

Eventually – a jagged beauticians'. The shopfront gone. But
two clean walls.

I dip a brush into rich black emulsion. Raise it, drip-
dripping… and paint what?

Anti-Assad slogans?

Do I tear him down, so that he can be replaced by the new
devils?

The holy-unholy monsters?

Drip drip.

A rich deep hatred rising.

For the foreigners, forcing me into ungodly alliance with
him, my Nemesis.

Drip drip.

I step back, and accidentally knock over the tin, its message
gagging unspoken into the silence of the rubble.

No paint? – no art.

I retreat towards the warm war-room of home through the
reshaped streets.

Wearing sticky black paint on my shoes. Obscured by pieces
of a crumbling city.

SEBASTIAN. My new house is the Most English House a tourist
could imagine. Thatched roof. Rose growing up the front.
Perfect country garden.

Bought with the smoulders of Kylie and Kanye.

Am on my lawn, waiting to watch sunrise over the orchard.
It's going to be a beautiful day.

The only blemish – a big slice of tree bark on the lawn.

I go to pick it up. Utter a shriek, and drop it in revulsion.

There are hundreds of woodlice underneath. Swarming.

Scuttling and scattering, through the garden, seeking
darkness.

And within seconds they're gone. Hiding in the cracks, in the
dark spaces. Armour-plated.

Invisible.

Hungry for the rot, of my English country garden.

NAMELESS. Nearly home. Rotors hack into my confusion.

A helicopter overhead.

A noisy, hovering Angel of Death.

Flying into my street.
A twitch of fear.
It'll be okay. It'll be okay.
Then I see it.
The falling bomb.
Spinning, graceful, languid. With fascinating beauty.
Like a high-board diver.
A compelling moment of dread calm.
Before the explosion of fury...
The ground shakes, I fall.
Then I find myself rising into thick bellowing mist.
Groping through the dense, intense fog of choking powdered concrete.
Which hides the Truth, the dreadful Truth that home
– that Home –
– is gone.

My distant voice, MOTHER!!!!
Tearing at smoking rocks of masonry, praying to her God.
Out of sync.
A time traveller from a distant future. On some frenzied archaeological dig. Discovering our ancient history in ruins.
Shards of a once-familiar crockery. Spikes of furniture.
Pieces of a mural: Adam's slack hand.
But God's fingers nowhere, nowhere, to be seen.
I am looking into ruin.
Unaware.
Not part of this world.
Unconnected.
When I should be looking out for the second bomb.
Which they always throw after the first, to take out the rescuers.
Oblivious, unseeing of the surprising rush of Hell that tosses me, on a dragonball of heat and dust.
Into deep, choking blackness.

SEBASTIAN. The rumbling roar of the crowd. Soccer Aid 2006. (*Roaring as if it's Wembley.*) Seventy-one thousand people inside Old Trafford. Maradonna is right there.

My job? Taking post-match pics of Robbie Williams with disabled kids.

Some in wheelchairs, some mentally impaired.

It's gloomy, low light. Must use the long lens, which'll fuck the depth of field. Can't get them all in focus.

Best to concentrate on the money shot. Sharp focus on the Robmeister.

But it's hard. One of the kids keeps making weird whale-noises, standing up, blocking Robbie.

Can't get a clean shot.

'Can we move that kid out of the picture. He's fucking it up.'

NAMELESS. A hospital corridor, as confused and as random as a beehive. Cries, screams, shouts of attention. An improvisation of nurses, a scatter of doctors.

I am the victim of a chemical attack.

Struggling for breath. Vomiting.

My hair will fall out, like the people in Ghouta.

The doctor with results.

'Good news. It wasn't a chemical attack.'

Thank God.

'Just morning sickness.'

'…What?'

'…The baby's unharmed.'

'Baby??'

'You're having a child.'

'…No, I'm not.'

'The results are categorical.'

'I can't be, I'm not. There's a mistake.'

'Would you like to see the paperwork?'

'Paperwork's wrong, check it, I cannot be compromised.'

'I can tell you with a hundred per cent certainty – '

'You're lying – you're trying to stop me fighting – you work for Assad! LIAR! LIAR!'

Nurses stop their duties.

'GET IT OUT OF ME.'

Doctors and porters coming running.

'KILL IT! KILL IT!'

Hands grabbing me, restraining holding.

'KILL IT!'

SEBASTIAN. Bin Laden's been shot.

Messenger and I were supposed to be having celebratory drinks.

But when he joins me, he doesn't seen in the mood to party. This man, who hadn't flinched whilst covering Rwanda, and the Tsunami – is on the verge of tears.

'I've just been made redundant. Along with a hundred other journos from the paper. Forty-two years in the industry: Over.'

'Fuck 'em John. You'll find a job elsewhere.'

He snorts into a pint.

'Where? They're all laying people off. The *Guardian*, the *Telegraph*. I'm a dying breed.'

'Be me next.'

He laughs cynically.

'*You'll* be alright. Always thought *I* was the Right-Time, Right-Place guy. But it's you. Taking pictures of Daniel Bedingfield, at the exact moment people stopped paying for news.'

He takes his frustrations out on a beermat.

'Know what's going to happen, don't you? Soon there won't BE any journalists. And all the papers will be written by the PR industry. Just cover-to-cover Star Wars Movies and Katie Price and your fucking mate Robbie Williams, all posing as news to sell us shit. All I know is, when you start giving Kim Kardashian's arse precedence over the suffering of millions, the West is fucked.'

(*Shrugs*.) 'It is what it is.'

His eye sockets deep in shadow.

'And it is food for Woodlice.'

Dusty shreds of beermat all over the table.

'We need to step up or we're going to lose all this.'

He sweeps the shreds over the table's brink.

NAMELESS. My mother claims me at the Hospital. She's alive. Was in the Church when the bomb fell. Praying.

Of course she praises His Benevolence and Mercy. Whilst ignoring the Wrath and Fury which destroyed her home in the first place.

We must dwell in the Church. Sleeping between the pews
with the dispossessed.

But my thoughts, here, are not holy.

I'm King Herod, planning a massacre of the innocent which
drains me, sapping my strength, my fire.

'This child is a gift,' smiles my mother.

'It's a Shabeeha. An enemy within. A parasite. I have
a DUTY, Mother.'

'You'll have to leave, you know. You can't raise a child
HERE.'

'How can I leave? Know how much it costs to be smuggled
to Europe? Can't even afford a loaf of bread.'

Can't leave, WON'T leave.

Here I am strong.

Here: I am the man with the shopping bags standing before
the tanks; the girl placing the flower in the barrel of a gun.

Leave? I'd be diminished: a painter, not an artist.

In the background the Priest, delivering a sermon: 'Blessed
are the children.'

I stand angrily. 'Fuck the children.'

SEBASTIAN. I have a name now. Am married to my second
wife, who was one of the many Sugababes.

And am having a retrospective of my work at the National
Portrait Gallery: 'Faces by Sebastian Nightingale'.

My agent's invited all my subjects to the launch.

Surprising how many turn up. Ed Sheeran, Katy Perry,
Pharrell, Kate Moss.

And Daniel Bedingfield...

(*Bedingfield*.) 'Hi!'

...at the fruit platter, stuffing apples into his pockets.

'Sebastian?'

'JOHNNY MESSENGER!'

Looking old. His teeth cadaverous from red wine.

'You're a celebrity, now.'

'Yes.'

'One "of them".'

'So. What are YOU working on?'

'Syrians in the Mediterranean.'

'Oh is that still going on?'

'More than ever. Six hundred thousand at the last count.'
I sense a lecture. Want to escape, but am blocked in by the
Pet Shop Boys.
'So what do you think?'
'Of these pictures?… Shit. Fucking shit. The lot of them.
Apart from that one,' he points at the Bin Laden, 'the only
one they'll still be hanging in a hundred years' time – '
' – I'd better go and mingle –'
'He fucking won you know. He wanted the division of the
communities and he got it. We did it for him. We built walls.
We built borders. Round our hearts. Round our minds. All
these desperate people, asking for our help – homeless, and
tortured – and we all start voting – the Americans, the Brits,
the French – we all start VOTING for them to FUCK OFF
AND DROWN.'
'This isn't the time or place John.'
'Oh sorry, I'm sorry, I'm so fucking sorry, I mean, God
forbid anybody talk about the issues.'
I grab Messenger by the arm, drag him through the crowd:
'This is my night, John, you have no right – '
'I believed in you. But you fucked off – '
Russell Brand sniggers, points, shares a joke with the
member-of-the-gallery-staff-he's-trying-to-fuck.
Messenger stares at him, directly:
' – you FUCKED OFF taking pictures of worthless wankers,
who because they hosted a Reality TV show think they're
Jesus.'
Russell Brand, for once, is speechless.

NAMELESS. Roaming the streets.
Seeking the sound of an oud.
Then I hear it, the warm metallic twang.
He sees me, is shocked.
'What happened to you?'
Suddenly aware of the filth in my clothes, 'They blew up my
house.'
'I'm sorry.'
Cold, wearing self-protection like a bulletproof vest.
'So what do you want? Paints?? The fight is lost, now. It's
all Jihadis.'

'…We need to talk.'

He itches at the oud's strings, like a scab.

(*Rifat*.) 'Nothing to talk about.'

'I'm pregnant.'

He looks from the oud. The music stops.

Stands. Raises a hand to my belly.

I chop it away.

'Don't. Don't touch me.'

'Do you know what sex it is?'

'Don't even know if I'm keeping it.'

(*Rifat appalled*.) 'You're its mother – it's your child – you protect it??'

'Exactly. I'm its mother, and I'm going to protect it from THIS world.'

'But the child would have us – '

Oh Rifat, Rifat, with his open face.

I try to picture him pushing the child in a swing. In a playground. Without big men with unsmiling faces.

I try to picture them holding hands, crossing the road, without looking at the rooftops.

I try to picture them with fingers with a full set of nails.

And I can't.

I can't.

Fragile. Too fragile.

The lonely swing. Contorting. Creaking.

'It… It's not yours.'

'What?'

'The child is not yours,' I say. 'I've made a mistake. It's not. It can never be yours.'

He shouts and shouts, as I walk off through collapsed buildings. Skeletal and dark.

SEBASTIAN. In the street. I shout and shout – then throw Messenger against the railings.

'You sanctimonious prick! Do you know why I'm not out in the Mediterranean with you, wearing my halo? Because I tried that, and no fucker would print the pictures.'

'So you do nothing…?'

Bono's having a crafty fag in a doorway. 'You okay, Sebastian?'

'Fine. Join you in a minute, mate.'
But he hangs round the door, enjoying the spectacle.
'Nothing's not an option, Sebastian. Nothing is
SOMETHING; Nothing's a choice. A political choice.
A hostile act of callousness. Nothing is the wedge between
the civilizations. Nothing is *Batman's* victory.'

He walks off into neon-lit streets.
Leaving me alone in the darkness.
Shouting into the void: 'Nothing?!!! NOTHING??? My
pictures of Atomic Kitten are NOT NOTHING!!'

Back in the party, the stars have ceased glittering, the celebs
have gone home.
The waiting staff, cleaning up. Scraps scraped into a bin,
shamefully loud.
Only Bedingfield left, still loitering at the buffet.
An apple falls out of his pocket.
I watch it bobble and roll.
Bruised fruit.

NAMELESS. Candlelight in the Church. Nervous shadows on
the wall.
The ordered repetition of prayer.
My mother carrying a candle, face flickering in nervous
flame. 'I have money to get you out.'
'What? How?'
'Took out a loan.'
'Against what?'
She's still.
Ever-strong, ever carrying the ramrod of faith in her spine,
Thrusts money: Dollars. Covered in engine grease.
'I work for the garage now.'
'Stinky Joram?? Mum!'
Now twitches, lurches; melting with liquid pain – and says:
'Mary Magdalene was one of Christ's greatest followers.'
'Can't take this.'
'It's not for you.'
She rubs the skin of my belly, the thin border between
herself and the grandchild she will never see.

'Not for you. For your masterpiece. The one inside.'
Then the draft flitters the flame like the wings of a dying
butterfly.

SEBASTIAN. Head pounding, chiming with the phone.
'...Hello?'
'Sorry.' It's Messenger.
'It's okay, John.'
'I didn't spoil the evening?'
'Not for me. But Bono thinks you're a bell-end.'
'Shit. I'm a bell-end's bell-end. Makes me the bell-end of
connoisseurs. The crème de bell-end.'
'See you, John – '
' – Wait. Got you a gig – A UN fact-finding mission in the
Med. Patrol boat seeking refugees...'
I sigh, mentally prepare excuses. No no no.
' – It's with Angelina Jolie.'
Yes yes yes.

NAMELESS. I must lose my city, my canvas. No more, my
hand liquid on the walls.
(*Mother*.) 'Smugglers are coming.'
My final work, myself.
I open my paints. Load my brush with cadmium scarlet.
And paint my lips.
(*Mother*.) 'Come on, pack!'
French Ultramarine to compliment my eyes.
Lamp Black my mascara.
(*Mother*.) 'Pack pack!'
I kneel before the mirror. Admire my work.
A last defiant assertion of human beauty.
(*Mother*.) 'Why aren't you packing?'
'I have everything I need.'

SEBASTIAN. To some, Angelina is a modern saint. Using her
fame to heal the world.
To others, she's a nutter, who collects vulnerable kids like
the Child Catcher from *Chitty Chitty Bang Bang*.
In truth, she has a fragility which I didn't expect of Lara Croft.
We meet on a boat off the coast of Samos.

'Hi I'm Angelina.' She says, unnecessarily.

'It's an honour. Seen all your movies. A big fan of
Malificent; thought *Girl, Interrupted* was great.'

'I appreciate you coming to cover this – '

' – and I saw *Mr & Mrs Smith* – '

'– it's a disaster of biblical proportions – '

'I quite liked Brad Pitt.'

' – I meant the refugee crisis.'

'Oh.'

Shows me cartoon-white teeth. Can almost hear them 'Ting'.

'Oh yes, sorry.'

'I admire your work, too. John showed me your Balochistan
pictures.'

(*Messenger, sneering.*) 'Yes, he was good *back then.*'

(SEBASTIAN *scowls.*)

The prow bumps uncomfortably over the waves.

NAMELESS. The hold of a rusting fishing vessel.

We've descended into Hell.

The skeletal tungsten of the single bulb, ghostly like an
X-Ray.

Each lurching wave produces screams,

Each crash strains my core.

The stench of vomit contagious.

Cramping in my gut.

Counting the seconds in my head

Each one bringing the journey closer to its end.

THUMP!

The screams desperate, *real*

Am lying in a nest of nets

Hoping that they'll absorb the waves' violence.

Instead my clothes absorb the

evil sloshing soup.

Of sick and piss and diesel.

THUMP!

And I fear each twisting crash may induce labour,

May have already induced labour;

Back aching stomach hardening

Cramping again.

THUMP!

AAAAAAH.

Please do not come now, baby bird.

My little one.

Stay inside, do not come into this world.

Not yet.

I will love you.

Protect you.

But not now.

Not into this world of piss and puke and pain.

THUMP!

AAAAAAH.

And suddenly a crack

A hole in the hull

waters rushing in

the boat splintering

dissolving into

oil and glass and wood

SEBASTIAN. Choppy seas, John's trying to find me the best
vantage point for the shoot.
'Is there any point me taking photos – seeing I was only ever
good "Back then"?'
A lurch in the waves.
'What happened to YOU, Sebastian? When we first met you
wanted to change the world. Now: I can only get you out
here if there's an A-List celebrity.'
'Couldn't take the pain of saving the world, John.'
Silence. A ferocious wave builds and builds before us. Then
Messenger turns on me, spittle and brine in the wind.
'No one asked you to save the world, Sebastian. Was asking
you to save yourself.'
Wave surging, higher higher.
'Humans are demigods. We have reason and compassion,
and creativity and empathy. And if the demigods don't use
those powers, they become just another animal: Ordinary.
That's YOU, Sebastian. For all your exhibitions and fame,
YOU have grown ordinary.'
The wave smashes on the deck in an explosion of spray.

NAMELESS. Mouthful of brine, gasping thrashing.
Flailing arms legs human flotsam.
AAAA
The child inside, tearing
Launching its own fight for life
I'm sorry little one
I tried, I tried
This is it, this is drowning.
Perhaps it's best you never came

SEBASTIAN. And as the wash of spray spreads over the deck
like realisation.
John towers above, feet sure, defying the winds.
'They threw Batman in the sea. They say he's Dead; but his
spirit's Alive. Sinking boats and drowning children. Dividing
between the communities. Because we all became
"Ordinary".'
My feet slipping, skidding.

I hear screams like on a rollercaster; a Doppler effect.
Rising and falling with the waves.
…A hand in the water!

NAMELESS. Consciousness fading
Darkness closing in.
Blue hands dragging my ankles into deep waters.
A noise… A boat!

SEBASTIAN. Must get the money shot, quick, get closer.
Angelina in front, the hand behind.
I slip skid. Washed with spray.
Scrabble upright.

NAMELESS. Hyperventilating
Hold on we can make it little one hold on

SEBASTIAN. A rope to my side. Coil it round my forearm.
To hold me to my task.
Boat lurches, it grips tighter.
Now Angelina falls.
No delicacy now.

Bold words frail in howling wind.
Rope bites tighter, won't let go.
Harder I struggle, Tighter it grips.
'Ordinary?'
No. No.
Looking past Angelina, waving her inside.
Pointing my lens at the girl in the water
Closing the aperture for greater depth

NAMELESS. Holdonholdonholdon.
Take my hand.
Take it!

SEBASTIAN. And I must get focus on those eyes.
The cover of *Time*, *Newsweek*. The Pulitzer.
Twisting the focus…
Twisting.

NAMELESS *and* SEBASTIAN. Twisted.

NAMELESS. And suddenly the wind is still,

SEBASTIAN. the waters calm,

NAMELESS. the surface a perfect mirror.

SEBASTIAN. Impossible to see who is in water,

NAMELESS. who is in air.

SEBASTIAN. And then the pull of a desperate tide and swell in
my chest

NAMELESS. Fingers weakening,

SEBASTIAN. camera slipping,

NAMELESS. spiralling towards brine.

SEBASTIAN. My voice rising, rolling, saying Help me,
Help me

NAMELESS. And I am straining with every fibre of my being.
Painting with sea and wind, and saying in a whisper as loud
as the waves:

My name is Farah. My eyes are blue.
And in my belly I carry the future.

Just take my hand.
Just take it.
Just take it.
JUST